Takumaru
Forex
Trading

By: Larry Jacobs

TABLE OF CONTENTS

TABLE OF CONTENTS

TABLE OF CONTENTS...2

NOTE TO READERS...4

INTRODUCTION...5

You can request more information here: 6

Chapter 1- INTERVIEW WITH TAKUMARU SAKAKIBARA.............7

Chapter 2- WHAT IS FOREX?...13

Chapter 3- JUST HOW DOES THE FOREX MARKET WORK?...........17

Chapter 4- WHEN DO YOU TRADE FOREX?.................................21

CHAPTER 5 – NEGATIVE THINKING 23

Chapter 6- MT4 CHARTING PLATFORM 29

Chapter 7 - BOLLINGER BANDS FIBO 31

Chapter 8 - TD SEQUENTIAL DMARK 34

Chapter 9 - MONTHLY CYCLES...36

Chapter 10 - DAYTRADING 5 – 30 MINUTE CANDLESTICKS.........37

Chapter 11- COUNTRY BANK RATES 44

CHAPTER 12 - WORLD CUP ADVISOR 45

Chapter 13 - OTHER BOOKS...48

CHAPTER 14 - 2015 WORLD CUP TRADING CHAMPIONSHIPS® SPONSORS: 66

ABOUT THE AUTHOR..68

DISCLAIMER...69

COPYRIGHT...70

F CONTENTS

_Toc430267615

NOTE TO READERS

Please remember that futures and forex trading involves significant risk of loss and is not suitable for everyone, and that past performance is not necessarily indicative of future results. World Cup Trading Championship (WCC) accounts do not necessarily represent all the trading accounts controlled by a given competitor. WCC competitors may control accounts that produce results substantially different than the results achieved in their WCC accounts. WCC entrants may trade more than one account in the competition.

For official WCC rules and information, visit http://www.worldcupchampionships.comAccounts trading in the WCC may be subject to commission rates different from those following the competitor's AutoTrade program. A trader's net return in the World Cup Championship will be higher than the program's net return in the WCA AutoTrade program due to a commission differential and the absence of subscription fees in contest calculations.

An investor must read, understand and sign a Letter of Direction for WorldCupAdvisor.com leader-follower programs before investing. This e-book contains statements of opinion.

INTRODUCTION

I want to thank you and congratulate you for downloading this book. This book contains an interview in Chapter 1 with Takumaru Sakakibara, who finished in 2nd place in the 2014 World Cup Championship of Forex Trading® with a 122.6% net profit. Takumaru's largest drawdown (cumulative peak-to-valley percentage decline in month-end net equity during the life of the account) was -52% from inception on 4-24-14 to 5-31-14. Please remember that past performance is not necessarily indicative of future results.

In the rest of the book I will explain to you some of the trading ideas Takumaru said he used in the championship. You can then actually see and understand how his ideas work.

I am not going to tell you exactly how Takumaru used the ideas to make his return of 122.6% on a $10,000 investment. That information is not public and belongs only to Takumaru.

I will tell you which indicators he used and help you understand how these indicators work. I would then recommend that you go to WorldCupAdvisor.com and consider following Takumaru's trades. You will be able to automatically mirror Takumaru's trades in your own brokerage account with World Cup Leader-Follower AutoTrade™ service. You will also be able to see what his trades look like on your own charts and better understand why he made the trades. There are no long-term commitments. You can subscribe month-by-month.

YOU CAN REQUEST MORE INFORMATION HERE:

http://get.worldcupadvisors.com/takumarutrading/

CHAPTER 1 - INTERVIEW WITH TAKUMARU SAKAKIBARA

Larry: What is your background before you started trading?

Takumaru: I graduated from Kwansei Gakuin University. I was in business a short period of time with Mizuho Securities and I was doing business with Sankyo securities. Currently I am engaged in the development of dealing and trading software in-house.

Larry: You placed second in the 2014 World Cup Championship of Forex Trading with a 122.6% net return on investment. Can you explain how you were able to achieve that?

Takumaru: I was able to achieve that by trading as usual.

Larry: What did you use for your ideas in your trading?

Takumaru: I mainly use three ideas in my trading.

Primarily, my investment style is to consider the difference in each country's interest rate. Then, I consider new positions that are expected to increase such interest differentials. For example, when U.S. interest rates are higher and Euro interest rates are lower, I consider selling the EUR/USD. Right now the U.S. interest rate is higher than the Euro, and that has made the Euro difficult to increase in price since last year.

I also consider deflection of the position as seen in the IMM. *(IMM stands for International Monetary Market a division of the Chicago Mercantile Exchange.)* Long and Short of Non-Commercials on the IMM shows the deflection of the position. Too much deflection of the position hinders price movements in that direction; it often accelerates the movement in the opposite direction.

For example, a large position of USD/JPY 100,000 Net Short of Non-Commercials is a negative signal.

Larry: That covers the first two ideas. What is the third?

Takumaru: Lastly, I consider the flow of the whole, for example the pension fund transfers by large cross-border enterprises. Stable financial flows is a factor that slowly moves the market if other factors are calm. For example, the deficit of Japan's ongoing trade balance will continue to weaken the yen. The corporate acquisition of funds of Japan is more than 10 trillion yen and that is a weak yen factor. If the pension funds of Japan continue purchases with the sale of one trillion yen per month then that will also continue to weaken the yen.

Larry: Do you use indicators?

Takumaru: I use Fibonacci and Bollinger Bands. I also use the 10-30 Average, the 5-10 Average and the 3-5 Average. In day-trading, I use resistance levels based on 5-minute and 30-minute candle charts. I always enter my trades in the direction of the main trend.

Larry: Do you use fundamentals?

Takumaru: I use the difference in each country's interest rate.

Larry: Do you use cycles or seasonality, and how?

Takumaru: I within monthly cycles.
For example, USD/JPY is likely to rise on the first Friday of the month, because so many people anticipate the employment data in the U.S. I like to buy USD/JPY in the last weeks of the month.

Larry: Do you use Commitment of Traders Report?

Takumaru: I don't use that report.

Larry: Do you trade anything else?

Takumaru: I trade stock, futures, and commodities.

Larry: How often do you trade?

Takumaru: I trade usually up to three times a day. I am both a day-trader and a long-term swing trader.

Larry: Are you affected psychologically by having others follow your trades on WorldCupAdvisor.com?

Takumaru: No I'm not.

Larry: Do you look at weather?

Takumaru: No I don't.

Larry: What services do you use, such as charting and news services?

Takumaru: I use MT4 charts and news from Reuters.

Larry: What would you advise traders to help them be successful?

Takumaru: Do not use high leverage. Also you should trade only when you have confidence in the market and never trade when you do not know the market.

Larry: Explain your trading style in some detail beyond "fundamental."

Takumaru: As I mentioned, my investment style is to consider primarily the difference in each country's interest rate. Then, I consider new positions that are expected to increase such interest differentials. For instance, the interest rate of the United States may be expected to rise on a certain date. On the other hand, Japan's interest rate may be expected to continue to be low due to the monetary easing policy from the Bank of Japan. Hence, I will examine possible entry avenues for the long USD/JPY. I will make an entry and adopt the business trading pattern in which one buys when the market rate is good and sells when it is not good. This is after taking into consideration the deflection of the position as seen in IMM as well as the flow of the pension fund and fund transfers by large cross-border enterprises.

Larry: How long might you hold onto a long-term position?

Takumaru: I hold onto a position about 3 to 12 months in my "home run" trades.

Larry: You trade stocks, futures, indices and FX... a lot of ground to cover, especially if your trading is 100% discretionary as you indicated. What are the challenges in jumping from one section to another?

Takumaru: Fluctuation factors are a big challenge. I started my trading with stocks. A price fluctuation of each stock can be impacted by the company's performance, demand and supply factors like buybacks, as well as the overall share price index.

Stock Price Index (SPI) is the measure used to monitor variation of stock prices and then compare that with competitors. SPI equals current market capitalization divided by market capitalization. All of the competitors do start with an SPI of 1000 in period 0. If SPI does increase then the company has then created shareholder value. SPI can be increased by then growing different segments of the existing markets or by then possibly investing in new markets successfully and then driving the costs down.

Share price index (SPI) is grouping a bunch of stocks in an industry together in a standardized way and that provides a window into a sector performance at a glance. Usually you then take the average of their prices to provide the idea how the industry is doing.

Stock price index (SPI) is an important factor of the price movement of individual stocks; I also got interested in stock index futures and started trading those. As for commodity futures, I was interested in physical gold, so I also dealt in it. I traded ETFs as they were becoming popular and highly correlated with the

Nikkei Stock Average. An ETF is an exchange traded fund which is a marketable security that tracks an index, commodity, bonds or a basket of assets like an index fund.

Stocks, futures, indices and FX all are interacting with each another. I often find a chance to get a profit by watching them as a whole. For example, gold and dollar are inversely correlated with each other. If dollar is not declining though gold is going up, it can be a predictor of depreciation of dollars.

Larry: It's quite an accomplishment to be able to survive as a full-time trader at such a young age. How have you been able to do it?

Takumaru: I think it was caused by the fact that I can program and I did not have to push myself as the standard of my ordinary life is not high. Basically, I make orders or final decisions at my own discretion, but for back tests, simulation, or collecting information, I often use programs.

Larry: Do you use price formations and how?

Takumaru: I will use break-outs from narrow ranges in long sideways periods of price action.

It is possible to earn a large return with a small risk by placing the stop loss on the opposite side of the range.

I use a number of candlesticks and TD sequentials (by Tom DeMark) which are my favorite.

Chapter 2- WHAT IS FOREX?

What is the forex market that Takumaru trades? Forex, or foreign currency exchange, is perhaps the biggest financial market in the world. It has an average daily turnover of nearly $5 trillion dollars. Forex is the exchanging of one currency for another one at its present exchange rate. The exchange is often done for the purposes of tourism and commerce. For example, say a person is travelling to Great Britain. He or she will exchange U.S. Dollars for British Pounds to pay for hotels, food and travel in Great Britain.

In the area of business the products that come from a different country need to be paid for. If a U.S. company needs to import a product from Great Britain it needs to pay in British Pounds. The exchange is done by United States or British banks.

The giant daily exchange of currencies that takes place creates a monetary opportunity, and that is forex trading. While a small percentage of FX transactions are done for exchange and payment purposes, a majority of FX trading is done for speculative purposes.

Banks use forex trading for monetary trading opportunities for their proprietary trading. They buy currencies with the hope that what they buy (called going long) will increase in value. Also the hope the currency they sell will get weaker or decrease in value (called going short).

The fluctuations between currencies are usually very small, but if you are dealing in big transactions the small price change in buying and selling currencies can result in large profits or losses. Leverage in forex trading, which is use of borrowed funds to facilitate transactions, can be as much as 50:1 in the U.S. That means that you can trade $50 of a major currency for each dollar deposited. This high degree of leverage magnifies both gains and losses.

The opportunity to make profits from trading currencies is used by many large multinational corporations and wealthy investors as well as hedge funds.

Forex trading is simply the basic process for buying and selling the many world currencies with the objective of making profit from the price differences. It is basically the idea of buying lows and selling highs of the different world currencies.

Here is a list of some of the currencies being traded:

Country – Currency - Symbol

United States – US Dollar - USD

Japan – Japanese yen – JPY

Great Britain – Pound – GBP

New Zealand – Zealand dollar – NZD

Switzerland – Swiss franc – CHF

Euro Zone Members – Euro – EUR

Canada – Canadian dollar – CAD

Australia – Australian dollar – AUD

You should learn the symbols of the currencies that are traded above if you are interested in trading the forex market.

When you trade the forex market you are trading pairs of the currencies. That is buying and selling currencies at the same time.

For example if you buy the British Pound with US dollars you are simultaneously selling the United States dollar and buying the British Pound.

Here is a list of some of the heavily traded currency pairs, often referred to as the "majors:"

GBP/USD
USD/CHF
AUD/USD
EUR/USD
USD/JPY
NZD/USD

Notice that in every one of these pairs the United States Dollar is on one of the sides. The U.S. dollar is called a reserve currency and is used in most international transactions. The EUR/USD is the world's most traded currency pair.

The Forex market is different from most other financial markets such as the New York Stock Exchange, which actually has a principal physical location. Forex is traded electronically within a vast network of banks and dealers around the world and it is done 24 hours a day, and five and a half days a week.

Speculators are those individuals and companies that buy and sell based on the price action. In fact, 90 percent of all trading is done by speculators. The volume from these speculators makes the market very liquid at any given time. Liquidity is very important in any market.

By using foreign exchange trading you may be able to make money trading at home or in your office at your own speed. It is a lot easier than it used to be. Foreign exchange trading or Forex for short has some advantages over other trading types such as stocks and futures. For example, there is deep market liquidity when trading major forex pairs.

Chapter 3- JUST HOW DOES THE FOREX MARKET WORK?

I want you to better understand the forex market so here are the two principals.

First when you buy a particular currency you believe that currency will get stronger and increase in value for a particular time frame over the currency you exchanged it for.

Second when you sell a particular currency you are thinking that currency will then weaken during a period of time against the one that you exchange it for.

The difference in prices of buying and selling is where your profit or loss comes from.

To illustrate that let's take the GBP/USD for example. Say you fully analyze the price action and reading the latest news you believe that the British Pound will increase in value against the U.S. dollar, so then you buy 15,000 British Pounds using United States dollars at a rate of 1.56000.

Buying 15,000 British Pounds = 23,400 U.S. dollars.

After then in a week, for example, you sell your British Pounds back to U.S. Dollars at the exchange rate of 1.57000.

Selling 15,000 British Pounds = 23,550 U.S. Dollars so you then have profit of 150 U.S. dollars.

Remember that trading the currencies is in pairs.

GBP/USD

The currency left is the base currency and the currency on the right side is the quote currency.

In the previous illustration you bought the British Pound and you had to pay 1.56000 U.S. dollars for each BP.

So when you buy you are buying (also known as "holding") the base currency and selling the quote currency.

Forex quotes are given in two prices – the bid price and the ask price.

The bid is the best available price another party is willing to pay for the base currency in a pair. The ask price is the best available price another party is willing to sell the base currency at.

Symbol – Bid – Ask

GBPUSD – 1.5612 – 1.5614

In this illustration the broker is willing to buy British Pounds at 1.5612 United States Dollars and willing to sell BPs for 1.5614 USD at the very same time.

The difference between the two prices is called the spread, and that is the fee the broker charges for facilitating the transaction. The spread is very small but when you are dealing in large quantities this can be very significant.

The movement in price is measured in what is called pips and pipettes. In many forex platforms, a pip (percentage in point) is the smallest fraction that a currency pair can move, and is also referred to as one basis point. However, some platforms also use pipettes, which equal one-tenth of a pip. In quotes which have 2 and 4 decimals, pipettes are expressed as the 3rd and 5th decimals, respectively. If the price in the British Pound moves from 1.56116 to 1.56117 then you have a move of one pipette.

The value of a pip fluctuation varies based on the quote currency and the position size.

It used to be that forex traded only in 100,000-unit lots, known as standard lots or standard contracts. That refers to 100,000 of the base currency. Now with the public in the market there are smaller lots available to trade.

Lots – Number of Units

Standard – 100,000

Mini – 10,000

Micro – 1,000

Nano – 100

Significant leverage is available in forex markets, as traders can borrow capital from the brokerage firms. The broker may require only what is called initial margin -- the amount a trader needs to initiate the position.

So if you want to trade a standard lot of 100,000 units of base currency, and the margin is just 1%, then you could put up as little as $1,000 to control $100,000.

This margin allows traders to make big profits with measured risk. However, employing leverage can also magnify losses so traders should always be mindful of their margin requirements, risk tolerances, and market events when trading.

Chapter 4- WHEN DO YOU TRADE FOREX?

Forex is traded on an enormous network of computers in different time zones.

So as a speculator when do you trade this market? To understand you need to know the various time frames.

Sydney opens the forex market on Sunday at 5:00pm
Tokyo opens two hours later.

Sydney and Tokyo close then at 2am and 4pm
London opens at 3am and ends at 12pm
New York opens at 8am and closes at 4pm.

The Japanese yen is the third most traded currency. At least 25% of transactions are with the Japanese Yen. To trade this market you might follow news coming out of Japan, China, New Zealand and Australia. There is a lot of price action with the AUD/JPY. The China news is very important.

The London open is the most active of all. At least one-third of all forex transactions happen at this time. This is a good time to trade as it can offer big opportunities. Trends established at this time may continue into the New York market. During this time the most active pairs to trade are the

USD/JPY
USD/CHF

EUR/USD
GBP/USD

During the New York session trades often continue direction from the London session. Most of these transactions happen with the USD pairs.

The timeframes with the most price action are generally during the six hours after Sydney opens and during the last five hours before New York closes.

CHAPTER 5 – NEGATIVE THINKING

For most people it is just simpler to be negative than to be positive.

We are in a society that does focus on what you don't have than rather what you do have.

If we then don't have what others have then it's easy for most of us just to call it everyone else's fault.

Many traders blame they losses on other people or a conspiracy against them.

These negative thoughts embed into our psyches cause us to dwell on everything bad in our lives. This hurts are ability to make good decisions for example following the rules of successful trading. What you need to do is to learn to turn off the bad thoughts and switch to the positive thoughts.

I am going to give you some tips and several exercises to help you remove these bad negative thoughts. I can't stress enough to be a successful trader you need to remove all negative thoughts. You need to infuse your mind with constructive positive thoughts and then it will allow you to experience contentment and success in your trading. You will then be inspired to be confident and take action at the right time and achieve success in trading.

Here are some tips and several exercises:

1) Reward yourself when you recognize a negative thought. What I mean is most of us don't recognize when we are being negative. Being negative is second nature for a lot of us. If you can identify when it occurs then you are on the way to correcting your way of thinking. The key to recognize a negative thought and turn it into a positive thing. Reward yourself for that. Identify the negative thought and stop it. Then tell yourself, "good catch"! That replaces the negative thought with a positive one.

2) You need to find what is best in other people. By doing this it will help you to be a positive person. You will not be judging people. That makes you negative. You know that everyone has many flaws, but it is your job to find what is positive in them and then target that positive thing. This will then make you feel much better about even yourself. This will help to make you a positive person and then actually a better trader.

Instead of having a head full of negative thoughts you will have only positive thoughts and that gives you a much better perspective on life and on things around you. You won't be over thinking trading situations and continuing to debate what you should do in a trading situation. You'll do what you are supposed to do. Over analyzing a trade will cause you to just doubt yourself and increase your perspective negatively. This will then prohibit you from making the right trading decisions when you need to make them.

You need to develop a good process of making the right trading decisions. You know the rules of correct trading. Write down the pros and cons of making a correct trade then take the proper action. The key is not being stuck in your uncertainty, inaction and over analysis.

3) Visualize Success. If you are all the time worrying about failing at trading you are setting yourself up for that failure. You need to replace this with a vision of success. See yourself making the right trading decision and making a profitable trade.

4) Develop a process to switch negative thoughts. When you get a negative thought ask yourself, "is this the way I want to feel?" Do you really want these negative thoughts in your life and potentially ruining your trading performance? You will never be happy with negative thoughts in your mind.

Here is an example:

Negative thought: I don't know how to handle what the market is doing right now?

Positive thought: This is my opportunity to learn how to trade this situation and learn something brand new.

When you are faced with conflicts you can comes to terms with it and create a positive outcome.

You need to develop many switches to turn negatives into positives. This will empower yourself. Write down the switches and continue to repeat them daily. In your trading you will get many curve balls that will make things difficult and turning a negative into a positive may seems impossible, but you can do it. Have confidence in yourself. Eventually you will have a more positive attitude over time and will find much more satisfaction in your trading and in your life.

To stay motivated can be a daily concern but you need to think about the benefits you will reap by just incorporating this way of thinking. Positive will do this for you:

a) You will be a positive person

b) You will have more satisfaction in life

c) You will be pleasant to be around

d) You will be content

e) You will believe in successful trading

f) You will build successful trading skills

g) You will have ability to adapt to different trading situations

h) You will reduce your stress and that will help your long term health

i) Your positive behavior will be contagious to others around you and they will be positive to you.

You need to keep in mind that if you have been negative for a long time it won't be easy to turn this around. You may have many years of negative thoughts in your head. But you can program your brain to make it positive and successful in trading. To have positive thinking will take a lot of time and practice. You must change your thoughts if you want to be successful in trading.

You should get a journal and start recording your journey. Write down your positive thoughts and the barriers that you need to break through. You will find it is much easier each and every day to be positive over time. Then after a while all the negative thoughts will disappear leaving your mind with positive thoughts and your will be a more happy person, a successful person and enjoyable to be around.

Another thing that will help you is to surround yourself with positive and successful people. You are really the average of the people that you spend the most time with. So when you start this changing of your negative thoughts it is important that you have supportive and positive people around you.

Psychologists have written many articles on how important it is to surround you with positive people. People need to reinforce your positive attitude. The way to do this is to take stock of 20 people who know and then ask what was their disposition and how did they make you feel when you were around them. Was it supportive for you? Were they positive or negative?

Choose the people that were positive and try to spend more free time with them over the next 90 days. These people will be the key for you to change your negative thoughts. Only you can take the responsibility for changing your life. You need to think positively no matter what the situation is.

I have covered what I see for you to be a more positive and a successful trader. You can unleash the infinite power inside of yourself and be a successful trader by thinking positive. You should take at least 10 minutes every day to implement what you have learned in this chapter to be positive.

I trust that you will now take the action you need to change your attitude to being positive and leverage this into being a successful trader. You can achieve anything you want or desire. It is my hope that you will look inside of yourself and commit to being positive and get the freedom that you will gain by ending any habit of being a negative person.

CHAPTER 6- MT4 CHARTING PLATFORM

MetaTrader 4 is the most popular Forex trading platform. You can download it here: This is the software that Takumaru uses.

http://www.metatrader4.com/en/download

After you download it and install it you will be prompted to open a free demo account. This account allows you to fully test many of the features of the platform.

The platform gives you unlimited number of charts plus 60 plus analytical tools. It allows you to copy deals of other traders and get news and alerts informing you of the important market events.

It also allows you to access and buy the largest market of trading robots and technical indicators.

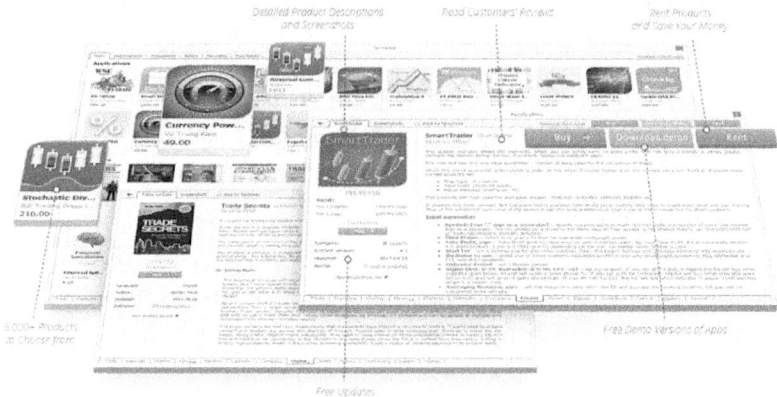

In this book I will explain only the indicators that Takumaru's uses such as:

1) The Bollinger Bands Fibo

2) The TD Sequential DMark

3) Select Moving Averages

CHAPTER 7 - BOLLINGER BANDS FIBO

The Fibonacci Bollinger Bands is what Takumaru uses and somewhat based on the same principals as the regular Bollinger Bands but instead of using standard deviation as its measure of volatility the Wilders Smoothed ATR is used in its place.

The middle band is the main moving average used to give you the intermediate-term trend. Then the 3 upper bands are then mathematically constructed by using the Wilders Smoothed ATR and multiplying it by each of the Fibonacci factors such as 1.681, 2.618 and 4.236 and then adding the results to the middle band. Then the other 3 lower bands are constructed the same way as the upper bands except the results are then subtracted from the middle bands.

You can download the Fibonacci Bollinger Bands from the forex factory.com

To then install it into the MetaTrader 4 platform locate and copy the indictor file on your computer. Open the data folder. Then open the indictors' folder and paste the file in it. Then simply restart MetaTrader4. Then open your MetaTrader 4 platform. Locate the Navigator panel. On the navigator find the custom indicators. Then click customer indictors and you should see the newly installed indicator. Simply then double click the indicator and the indicator properties window will appear. Then click OK.

Here is how to use the system:

First place the Bollinger Bands on the chart and then locate point 1 and point 2. For either long or short positions both of the points need to be outside of the Bollinger Bands. Point 3 needs to be then inside of the Bollinger Bands.

Point 3 must retrace between 38.2% and 61.8% of the price swing between point 1 and 2.

A long setup requires a move from a swing point low to a swing point high and then a retracement to a low.

Go long if the market moves up to this level:

Subtract point 1 from point 2 and divide the difference and add it to point 3.

If you are long 2 units then exit both of them at the initial stop which is point 3 minus one point.

Use a trailing stop if it moves higher by finding the highest close and subtract 25% of the difference between point 1 and 2.

Target 1 is calculated by adding point 3 to target 2 and divide by 2.

Target 2 is calculated by adding point 2 to point 3 and subtracting point 1 from the total.

Chapter 8 - TD SEQUENTIAL DMARK

Technical analysis tools developed by Thomas Demark have an excellent reputation from market technicians from around the world. This is one of the best tools that Takumaru uses in this trading. Many traders believe that the TD Sequential is 70% to 90% accurate. The software add-on is available for MetaTrader 4. This is one of Takumaru's favorite tools.

The TD Sequential Indicators automatically recognize and even will display the TD Sequential indicators every day. This is very cool. It identifies when a trend is just starting or when it is then finally exhausted and which day to enter a new position or to exit one. This ability of the indicator makes it stand out from others.

There is a lot more to this tool, but the explanation is limited here due to copyright of the developer Tom DeMark. For more information on how to more fully use it please contact DeMark Analytics, LLC.

Here are the basic signals using the software:

TD Setup

You get a buy signal when you have 9 consecutive price bars that are then less than the closes of the 4 price bars earlier.

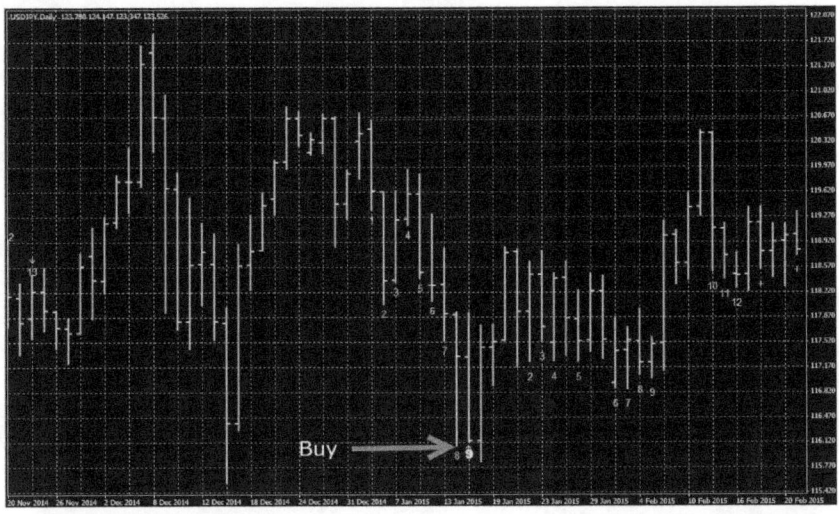

You get a sell signal when you have 9 consecutive price bars closes that are greater than the close of 4 price bars earlier.

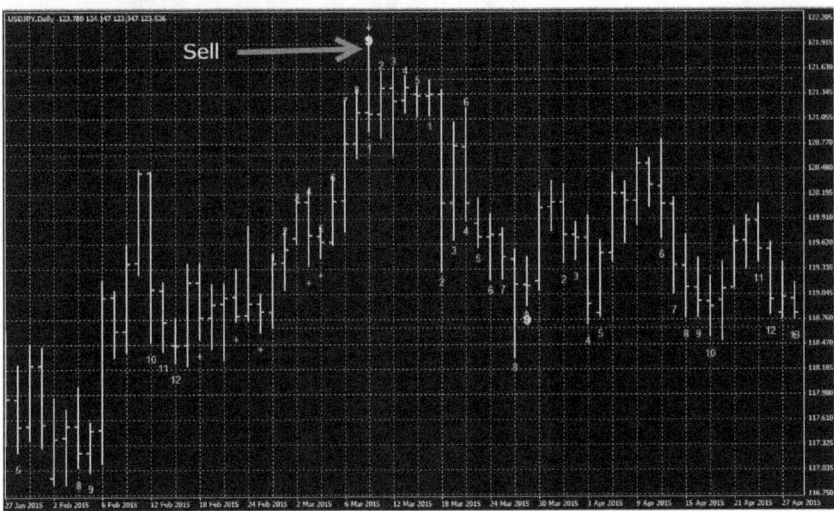

CHAPTER 9 - MONTHLY CYCLES

Larry: Do you use cycles or seasonality's and how?

In the interview Takumaru buys the USD/JPY in the last weeks of the month. Using Market-Analyst you can set that up on the charts for illustration purposes. Notice the market almost always rallies in the last weeks of the month.

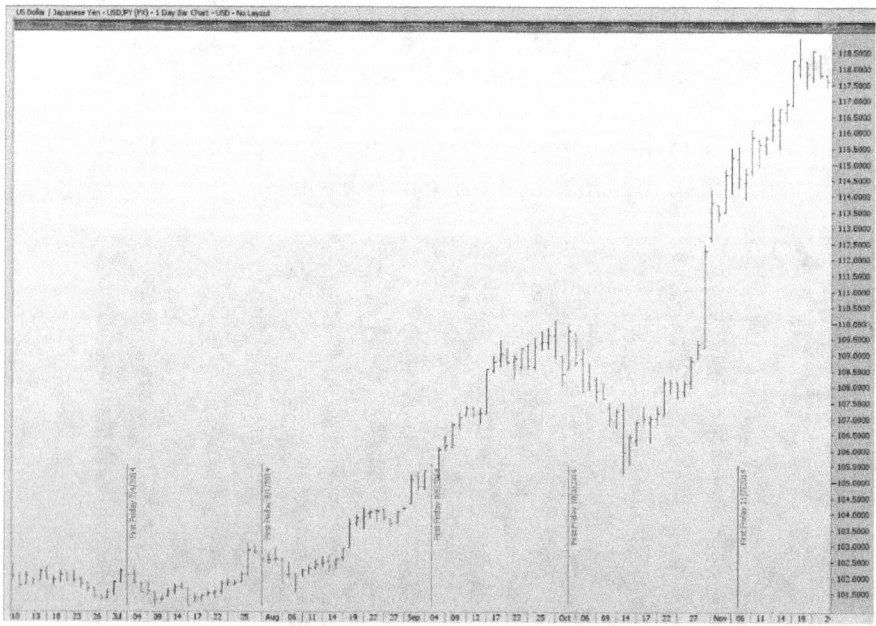

CHAPTER 10 - DAYTRADING 5 – 30 MINUTE CANDLESTICKS

In day trading, Takumaru does what he calls resistance trading based on the 5 minute and 30-minute charts using candle charts to indicate trend direction.

Basically when these moving averages cross they then form resistance. Takumaru trades the 10-30 average. See next chart.

He also trades the 5-10 average, See next chart.

And finally the 3-5 average. See the next chart.

He uses the 5-minute chart as a trigger using the 30-minute chart as the main trend. You can always trade with the main trend using 30-minute charts and then use the 5-minute charts to get in using the following candlestick patterns. See the following chart the 30-minute is on the left and the 5-minute is on the right.

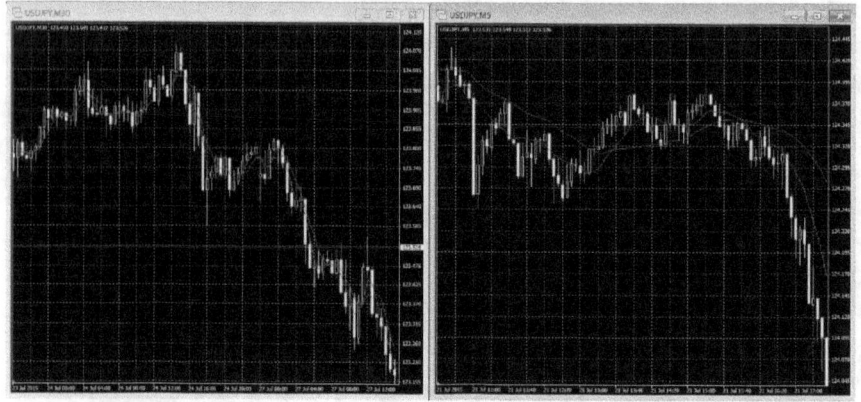

You need to memorize these basic but very important candlestick patterns.

Doji – Bears and Bulls are in indecision

Bullish Engulfing Pattern – Found at the end of a downtrend

Bearish Engulfing Pattern – Found at end of uptrend

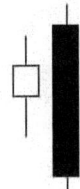

Dark Cloud Cover – Found at end of uptrend

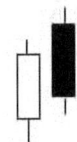

Gravestone Doji – Found at market bottoms and tops.

Long Legged Doji – Found at market tops

Piercing Pattern – Bottom Reversal

Hammer and Hanging-Man Found at tops and bottoms

Morning Star – A bottom reversal

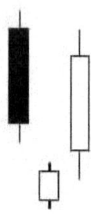

Evening Star – Found at end of uptrend

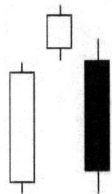

Shooting Star – Top is near

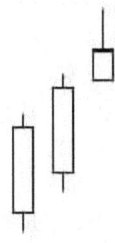

Chapter 11- COUNTRY BANK RATES

In the interview Takumaru said this: "My investment style is to consider primarily the difference in each country's interest rate. Then, I consider new positions that are expected to increase such interest differentials. For instance, the interest rate of the United States may be expected to rise on a certain date. On the other hand, Japan's interest rate may be expected to continue to be low due to the monetary easing policy from the Bank of Japan. Hence, I will examine possible entry avenues for the long yen-dollar. I will make an entry and adopt the business trading pattern in which one buys when the market rate is good and sells when it is not good. This is after taking into consideration the deflection of the position as seen in IMM as well as the flow of the pension fund and fund transfers by large cross-border enterprises."

You can find the interest rates for each country here:

http://www.tradingeconomics.com/country-list/interest-rate

CHAPTER 12 - WORLD CUP ADVISOR

About http://www.worldcupadvisor.com/

Talented professionals from around the world display their live futures and forex trading accounts in real time on WCA and allow subscribers to follow their activity. You can follow the trading of any WCA lead account automatically in your own account with World Cup AutoTrade service. Program features include:

Transparency:

All trades displayed on WorldCupAdvisor.com are actual trades in funded accounts unless otherwise noted. Details of every round-turn trade made in every available account are shown in the Advisor Performance section; for a free login, complete the "Create Your FREE Guest Login" form on the home page. Profit/loss in the Advisor Performance section is shown exclusive of commissions, fees, transaction and subscription costs; to evaluate the impact of these trading overhead costs, click the Net-Profit Calculator link. Detailed Performance Reports are also available within the Advisor Performance section. Read about each advisor and the specifications of his lead ("Live Update") accounts in the Advisors section. Our lead traders compete with each other to earn customer trust and subscription business.

Clarity:

Subscribers have access to a real-time display of activity in the lead account(s) to which they are subscribed. Displays feature separate screens for orders entered, open positions, closed positions and advisor commentary (please note that some order screens are disabled upon request of the advisor). When you're logged into a Live Update program, an instant message will appear on your screen and a bell will ring any time there is new activity. An email notification also accompanies each new activity, and subscribers can also receive text message notifications if desired at no additional charge.

Flexibility:

Subscriptions are sold on a month-to-month basis, eliminating long-term commitments. With AutoTrade service, subscribers can start a new program or stop an existing one with a single phone call. Subscribers can control their own leverage by adjusting funding levels and adding or reducing exposure to a variety of programs.

Diversification:

The wide variety of WCA accounts gives investors the opportunity to diversify across asset classes, trading products and strategies. Please note, however, that diversification in not necessarily available when trading a single program. Click here to learn more about ways you can diversify your WCA investments. A prospect should evaluate each specific program's specifications to determine whether or not that program is suitable to the individual based on that person's diversification requirements. Monthly subscriptions are sold separately for each program.

Confidence:

We try hard to identify traders we believe are capable of sustaining profitable performance on a net basis over time. Many of our advisors have posted top finishes in the prestigious World Cup Trading Championships®. We also feature accounts traded by noted system developers, authors, commentators and educators. The WCA live trading "incubator" is an active testing ground for new programs. WCA AutoTrade service is designed to deliver same-price fills for leader and followers alike on futures trades; authorized brokers will waive commissions on any WCA leader-follower trade in which a follower's fill price is not equal to or better than the lead trader's fill price (with the exception of trades placed outside a program's AutoTrade block when synchronizing positions for a follower entering a program or liquidating positions for a follower exiting a program).

Risk and suitability:

It is important to remind you that trading futures and forex involves significant risk of loss and is not suitable for everyone. Following any of our lead accounts should be undertaken with risk capital only. Before investing, you should carefully consider your risk tolerance and suitability for this type of investment.

Support:

We're here to answer your questions and provide a personal tour of the site if desired. Contact us by email at info@worldcupadvisor.com or by phone at 1-312-454-5000 or 1-877-456-7111.

CHAPTER 13 - OTHER BOOKS

Guide to Successful Online Trading: Secrets from the Pros

http://www.amazon.com/Guide-Successful-Online-Trading-Secrets-ebook/dp/B00QOBED34

This is one of the finest trading books you'll ever see about trading. The reason is that it comes from a group of expert pro traders with multiple years of experience.

Trading as you know is extremely difficult. It is estimated that 90% of traders lose money in the markets. To help you overcome this statistic, the pro traders in this book give you their ideas on trading with some of the best trading methods ever developed through their long time experience. By reading about these trading methods and implementing them in the markets you will then have a chance to then join the ranks of the 10% of the successful traders.

The traders in this book have through experience the right attitude and employ a combination of technical analysis principles and strategies to be successful. You can develop these also.

Trading is one of the best ways to make money. Apply the trading methods in this book and treat it as a business. The purpose of this book is to help you be successful in trading.

From this book you will get all the strategies, Indicators and trading methods that you need to make big profits in the markets.

This book gives you:

1) Audio/Visual Links to presentations from pro traders

2) The best strategies that the professional traders are using now

3) The broad perspective you need in today's difficult markets

4) The Exact tools that you need to make profitable trading decisions

5) The finest trading education

I wish to express my appreciation to all the writers in this book who made the book possible. They have spent many hours of their time and hard work in writing their section of the book and the putting together their video presentation for the online expo.

Trade the Markets with an Edge: Use Your Mind

http://www.amazon.com/Trade-Markets-Traders-World-Online-ebook/dp/B00KTQJV50

If you don't have the mind of a top trader, this book might be able to help you develop one. The writers in this book are very experienced and they are here to help you to be successful. Each of them has their own expertise in trading. What you need to do is to read the entire book and find the trader that fits your own trading style and grab it and make it your own. It is just that simple.

Find Success

This book presents to you the best trading strategies of these traders so that you might be able to select those that fit you best and then implement them into your own trading style.

In this book you'll learn:

1) How these expert traders make money and why

2) How to develop your own trading strategy

3) How to improve your trading psychology

4) How to be the trader you always wanted to be. You'll also learn how to avoid the losers and get rid of emotional attachment to trades. To be successful you need to learn to dump the losers quickly and keep the winners for big moves. Another thing this book does it that it gives you the desire to make continuous profits just like the master traders do.

Making profits one after another gives you a fantastic feeling which is tremendous!

Tips for Success

Also in this book you will know who to listen to for ideas from people who have many years of experience and who are seasoned traders.

Crucial Factors

In this book learn about crucial factors in the markets that many experts won't tell you about regarding time, volume and little known indicators. You'll know the right factors that can make you a profitable trader. The unique viewpoints from these many traders can explain why many traders lose and that can help you. The book was designed to help you develop your own trading edge in the markets to put you above others who don't have an edge and just trade by the seat of their pants.

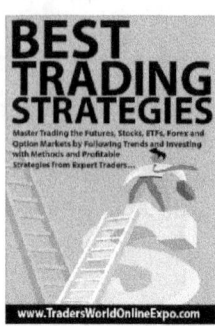

Best Trading Strategies

http://www.amazon.com/Best-Trading-Strategies-Futures-Markets-ebook/dp/B00GG94F78

This is one of the most fascinating books that was ever written about trading because it is written by over thirty expert traders. These traders have many years of experience and they have learned how to turn technical analysis into profits in the markets. This is extremely difficult to do and if you have ever tried to trade the markets with technical analysis you would know what I mean. These writers have some of the best trading strategies they use and have the conviction and the discipline to act assertively and pull the buy or sell trigger regardless of pressures they have against them. They have presented these strategies at the Traders World Online Expo #14 in video presentations and in this book.

What sets these traders apart from other traders? Many think that beating the markets has something to do with discovering and using some secret formula. The traders in this book have the right attitude and many employ a combination of fundamental analysis, technical analysis principles and formulas in their best trading strategies.

Trading is one of the best ways to make a lot of money in the world if one does it right. One needs to find successful trading strategies and implement them in their own trading method. The purpose of this book is to present to you the best trading strategies of these traders so that you might be able to select those that fit you best and then implement them into your own trading.

I wish to express my appreciation to all the writers in this book who made the book possible. They have spent many hours of their time and hard work in writing their section of the book and the putting together their video presentation for the online expo.

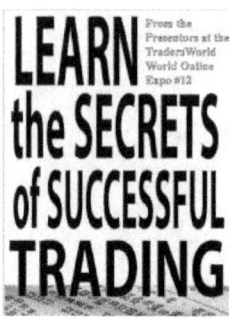

Learn the Secrets of Successful Trading

http://www.amazon.com/Secrets-Successful-Trading-Traders-Online-ebook/dp/B00A2ZIJQ0

Learn specific trading strategies to improve your trading, learn trading ideas and tactics to be more profitable, better optimize your trading system, find the fatal flaws in your trading, understand and use Elliott Wave to strengthen your trading, position using correct sizing to trade more profitable, understand Mercury cycles in trading the S&P, get consistently profitable trade setups, reduce risk and increase profits using volume, detect and trade the hidden market cycles, short term trading by taking the money and running, develop your mind for trading, overcoming Fear in Trading, trade with the smart money following volume, understand and use the Ultimate Oscillator, use high power trading with geometry, get better entries, understand the three legs to trading, use technical analysis with NinjaTrader 7, use a breakout system with cycles for greater returns with less risk, use Turn Signal for better entries and exits, trade with an edge, use options profitably, learn to trade online, map supply and demand on charts, quantify and execute portfolio rotation for auto trading.

Written by Many Expert Traders

The book was written by a large group of 35 expert traders, with high qualifications, most of who trade professionally and/or offer trading services and expensive courses to their clients. Some of them charge thousands of dollars per day for personal trading! These expert traders give generally 45-minute presentations covering the same topics given in this book at the Traders World Online Expo #12. By combining their talents in this book, they introduce a new dimension to finding a profitable trading edge in the market. You can use ideas and techniques of this group of experts to leverage your ability to find an edge to successfully trade. Using a group of experts in this manner to insure your trading success is unprecedented.

You'll never find a book like this anywhere! This unique trading book will help you uncover the underlying reasons for your lack of consistency in trading and will help you overcome poor habits that cost you money in trading. It will help you to expose the myths of the market one by one teaching you the right way to trade and to understand the realities of risk and to be comfortable with trading with market. The book is priceless!

Parallels to the Traders World Online Expo 12

The articles in this book exactly parallel the video presentations given at the Traders World Online Expo #12. This expo joins these top trading experts together with active traders looking for trading strategies & specific recommendations to help them profit

in the markets and is held online at
TradersWorldOnlineExpo.com.

From the DVD you'll learn: Time and Price Points; Consistently
Profitable Trade Setups; How to Control Fear of Trading;
Detecting and Trading Hidden Market Cycles; Position Sizing;
Detailed Analysis of the S&P Market, 3 Keys to be a System Trader,
Trading with an Edge, Lift off Trading Systems, Monetizing your
Trading Expertise; Tracking Smart Money; Trading Price Cycles,
Using Options, Mastering Trading with NinjaTrader; Learning
Andrews Trading and much more.

Finding Your Trading Method

http://www.amazon.com/Finding-Trading-Method-Traders-Online-ebook/dp/B00DAIOL0E

Finding your trading method is the main problem you need to solve if you want to become a successful trader. You may be asking yourself, can I find my own trading method that will reflect my own personality toward trading? For example, do you have the patience to sit in front of a computer and trade all day? Do you prefer to swing trade from 3-5 days or do you like to hold positions for weeks and even months? Every trader is different. You need to find your own trading method.

Finding out your trading method is extremely important to produce a profitable benchmark that can be replicated in your live account. Perhaps the best way to find a successful trading method is to listen to many expert traders to understand what they have done to be successful. The best way to do that is to listen to the Traders World Online Expos presentations. This book duplicates what these experts have said in their presentations, which explains what they have done to find their own trading method.

If you have a trading method that gives you a predictable profit, then that type of objectivity contributes to your trading edge. The problem with most traders is that being inconsistent will never allow them to have an edge. After you find your trading method that you feel comfortable with, you must have the following:

An overall plan to:

1) Set your rule set and plan and then stick with it in all of your trading.

2) To give you a trading plan for every day.

The trade plan then should:

1) Have an exact entry price

2) Have a stop price

3) Have a way to add positions

4) Tell you where to take profits

5) Have a way to protect your profits

By reviewing all the methods given in this book by the expert traders, it will give, you the preliminary steps that you need to find your footing in finding your own trading method.

Reading this book and by seeing the actual recorded presentations on the Traders World Online Expo site can act as a reference tool for selecting your method of trading, investment strategies and tactics.

It took many of these expert traders in this book 15 – 30 years to finally come up and find the answers to find their trading method to make consistent profit. Finding your trading method could be then much easier when you read this book and incorporate the techniques that best fit your personality and style from these traders. This book will enable you to that fastest way to do that.

So if you want help to find your own trading method to be successful in the markets then buy and read this book.

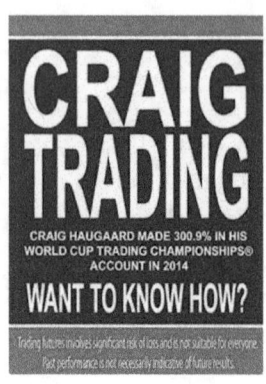

CRAIG TRADING: Craig Haugaard made 300.9% in his World Cup Trading Championships® Account in 2014 - Want to Know How?

http://www.amazon.com/CRAIG-TRADING-Haugaard-Trading-Championships%C2%AE-ebook/dp/B00WT2CO7Y

This book contains an interview that I made with Craig, the third-place finisher in the 2014 World Cup Championship of Futures Trading® with a 300.9% net profit. I asked him many questions on exactly how he did it.

In the rest of the book I explain to you how to use the indicators that Craig used to make his 300.9% return. Always remember that trading futures and forex involves significant risk of loss and is not suitable for everyone, and that past performance is not necessarily indicative of future results.

Here are the indicators that he used:

• Seasonality

• MACD

- Stochastics

- Moving Averages

- Trailing Stops

- Fibonacci Retracements & Extensions

All of the charts in this book are produced using my favorite charting software Market-Analyst®. I have also arranged for you to get a FREE trial so that you might have the chance to actually work with these indicators with a real charting platform. A link to the free trial is in the book.

You will also be able to view the video presentations that I personally created so you can see how these indicators can be setup and followed with clear and concise step-by-step instructions.

After you understand how these indicators work, I would then recommend that you go to WorldCupAdvisor.com and consider following Michael Cook's real-time trades.

This one-of-a-kind book teaches you how to identify the direction of the markets and trade the markets by using popular trading indicators. This is done by concise instructions backed by learning videos, hands on practice with real trading software and by following real-time trades of a master trader.

Michael Cook won the
2014 World Cup Championship
of Futures Trading® with a

366% net profit

michael

trading

Learn about some of the
trading tools he used

Trading futures involves significant risk of loss and is not suitable for everyone.
Past performance is not necessarily indicative of future results

http://www.amazon.com/Michael-Trading-Learn-about-trading/dp/1515208729

Michael Cook was the first-place finisher in the 2014 WORLD CUP Championship of Futures Trading® with a 366% net profit. In this book there is a detailed interview with Michael with questions and answers of exactly what he used to win the championship. In this book I will explain to you the indicators that he said he used in the interview. You can then actually see and understand how they work. Here are some the indicators and methods that he said he used: 1) Moving Averages 2) Seasonality 3) Cycles 4) Seasonality 5) Price Patterns 6) William's %R 7) Long with Stops 8) Commitment of Traders Report You will also be able to download a video presentation that I personally created so you can see how these indicators can be setup and followed in a step-by-step manner. After you understand how these indicators work, I would then recommend that you go to WorldCupAdvisor.co and consider following Michael Cook's trades.

Please keep in mind that trading futures and forex involves significant risk of loss and is not suitable for everyone, and that past performance is not necessarily indicative of future results.

Traders World Online Ex

http://www.amazon.com/Mastering-Your-Trading-Advisors-Traders/dp/1515176886

"Mastering Your Trading" is the perfect source for learning various methods of trading the market from expert advisers. This book focuses on various methods of trading developed by many top trading advisors. There are 17 well written articles and it is packed by insight that can benefit the beginning to the expert trader. This is a must read. The trading methods and strategies presented in this book can help to succeed in today's volatile market environment. From preparing your psychology to the demands of timing the market and managing the risk, this book tells it all. The book provides you the tools that are necessary for making the right trades and when to get in and out of the market. The book covers:

• Price and Volume the only True Indicators

• Uncovering Market Secrets • How to handle capital exposure

• Secrets of Safe Profitable Day Trading

• Using Social Media Sentiment Cycles

• How to Dramatically Improve Your Trading Psychology

• How to Handle Trading Losses

• Using a Market Scanner to Save Time

• How to Stop Guessing

• How to Get the Right Trading Computer

• Simple and Practical Trading Tips

• And much more... This book is an enhanced Edition which means that the articles are backed with audio visual presentation links. Most of the presentations are in HD quality and are put together by the writers of the articles in the book and really help the learning process. Successful trading is based on knowledge and having the right psychology to trade the markets. This book will lift your trading to a much higher level and will save you an enormous amount to time.

CHAPTER 14 - 2015 WORLD CUP TRADING CHAMPIONSHIPS® SPONSORS:

ONLINE TRADING ACADEMY

http://www.tradingacademy.com

OTA is the world's most trusted name in financial education for stocks, forex, futures and options.

APEX INVESTING INSTITUTE

http://apexinvesting.com

THE source for how to trade Futures, Forex, CFD's and NADEX Binaries and Spreads

TRADE NAVIGATOR

http://www.tradenavigator.com

The Trade Navigator Trading Platform takes immense quantities of complex data and distills it down to what really matters.

THE BUBBA SHOW

http://thebubbashow.org

Learn the intricacies of options trading from Todd "Bubba" Horwitz, educator, trading coach and author OF "AVERAGE JOE OPTIONS."

WORLDCUPADVISOR.COM

http://www.worldcupadvisor.com

Automatically mirror the trading of futures and forex professionals with World Cup Leader-Follower AutoTrade™ service.

NINJATRADER

http://www.ninjatrader.com

Award-winning software that benefits all levels of traders with trade management advanced charting, market analytics, customizable features and more.

ABOUT THE AUTHOR

Larry Jacobs has a B.S. and Master's Degree in Business and has been editor of Traders World Magazine since 1988. It's a leading financial magazine which has both classical and modern technical analysis articles as well as reviews of the latest trading books, trading computer hardware and software.

He also has written dozens of articles on how to setup your home trading office and how to get the right trading computer.

He is author of several trading books including Gann Masters, Gann Masters II, Gann Master Charts Unveiled, Patterns and Ellipses and W. D. Gann in Real Time Trading. Gann Masters was so popular it was recently translated in to Italian.

He has reviewed almost every trading software program available and has interviewed and talked to the many of leading traders of the world.

He won the World Cup Championship of Stock Trading® in 2001.

DISCLAIMER

This publication is intended to provide helpful and informative material. It is not intended to give trading recommendations nor is it to replace the advice of a financial advisor. No action should be taken solely on the contents of this book. Always consult your financial advisor on any matters regarding your investing or trading before adopting any suggestions in this book or drawing inferences from it.

The author and publisher specifically disclaim all responsibility for any liability, loss or risk, personal or otherwise, which is incurred as a consequence, directly or indirectly, from the use or application of any contents of this book.

Any and all product names referenced within this book are the trademarks of their respective owners. None of these owners have sponsored, authorized, endorsed, or approved this book.

Always read all information provided by the manufacturers' product labels before using their products. The author and publisher are not responsible for claims made by manufacturers.

Trading futures and forex involves significant risk of loss and is not suitable for everyone. Past performance is not necessarily indicative of future results. There is unlimited risk of loss in selling options. An investor must read, understand and sign a Letter of Direction for WCA programs before investing. There are no guarantees of profit no matter who is managing your money. Net-profit data under "Leaders to Follow" and "Top Net

COPYRIGHT